JOHN ROTHENSTEIN

EDWARD BURRA

PENGUIN BOOKS

THE PENGUIN MODERN PAINTERS

Editor Sir Kenneth Clark

Made and Printed in Great Britain by George Pulman & Sons Ltd.
The Cranford Press, London and Wealdstone, Middlesex
Colour Plates by W. F. Sedgwick, Ltd.

Published by
Penguin Books Limited
Harmondsworth, Middlesex, England
1945

COLOUR PLATES

Plate 1   FORTUNE TELLERS (1929), $22\frac{1}{2} \times 31$, *water-colour*; owned by the Artist

Plate 3   THE TORTURERS (1935), 30×22, *water-colour*; owned by John Rothenstein, Esq.

Plate 5   ROSSI (1930), 24×20, *water-colour*; owned by the Artist

Plate 7   LES FOLIES DE BELLEVILLE (1928), $24 \times 19\frac{1}{2}$, *water-colour*; owned by the Artist

Plate 9   THE TERRACE (1927), 24×20, *water-colour*; owned by Mrs. H. Walston

Plate 11   HARLEM (1936), 31×22, *water-colour*; owned by The Tate Gallery

Plate 13   THE POINTING FINGER (1937), 31×22, *water-colour*: owned by the Artist

Plate 15   ON THE SHORE (1934), $19\frac{1}{4} \times 24\frac{1}{4}$, *water-colour*; owned by John Rothenstein, Esq.

Plate 17   CAMOUFLAGE (1938), 40×81, *water-colour*; owned by Redfern Gallery and Mrs. Keswick

Plate 19   THE PUPPET (1937), 40×30, *water-colour*; owned by the Artist

Plate 21   LANDSCAPE WITH WHEELS (1937), 19×24, *water-colour*; owned by Robert Helpmann, Esq.

Plate 23   BLUE-ROBED FIGURE UNDER TREE (1937), $46\frac{1}{2} \times 31$, *water-colour*; owned by the Artist

Plate 25   SOLDIERS (1942), $41\frac{1}{2} \times 81\frac{1}{2}$, *water-colour*; owned by The Tate Gallery

Plate 27   MEXICAN CHURCH (1938), $51\frac{1}{2} \times 40\frac{3}{8}$, *water-colour*; owned by The Tate Gallery

Plate 29   BAL DES PENDUES (1937), 62×43, *water-colour*; owned by the Artist

Plate 31   WAR IN THE SUN (1938), 40×80, *water-colour*; owned by the Artist

BLACK AND WHITE PLATES

Plate 2   LIFE STUDY (1924), 15 × 11, *pencil drawing*; owned by the Artist

Plate 4   DANCING GIRLS IN TOP HATS (1928), 22 × 14½, *pen and ink drawing*; owned by the Artist

Plate 6   NIGHT CLUB (1930), 13 × 16½, *pencil drawing*; owned by John Rothenstein, Esq.

Plate 8   THE SISTERS (1929), 24 × 19, *oil*; owned by the Artist

Plate 10   DANDIES (1930), 13 × 10, *pencil drawing*; owned by John Rothenstein, Esq.

Plate 12   JOHN DETH (1932), 22 × 30, *water-colour*; owned by Conrad Aiken, Esq.

Plate 14   DANCING COWS (1933), 24 × 19, *water-colour*; owned by Miss B. Dawson

Plate 16   THE CAFÉ (1932), 30 × 25, *water-colour*; owned by Desmond Ryan, Esq.

Plate 18   DUENNAS (1934), 22 × 17½, *water-colour*; owned by Miss B. Dawson

Plate 20   SILENCE (1936), 46 × 31, *water-colour*; owned by the Artist

Plate 22   BLASTED OAK (1937), 25 × 29, *water-colour*; owned by C.E.M.A.

Plate 24   HOLY WEEK: SEVILLE (1938), 66 × 33, *water-colour*; owned by the Artist

Plate 26   THE VISION OF ST. THERESA (1938), 43 × 30, *pencil drawing*; owned by the Artist

Plate 28   THE WAKES (1937), 40¼ × 27½, *water-colour*; owned by The Tate Gallery

Plate 30   THE RIOT (1939), 30½ × 44, *water-colour*; owned by the Artist

Plate 32   AGONY IN THE GARDEN (1936), 30½ × 44, *water-colour*; owned by the Artist

EDWARD BURRA

EDWARD JOHN BURRA, the son of Henry Curtis Burra—a solicitor who retired as a relatively young man to his small property near Rye—was born on March 29th, 1905, at 31, Elvaston Place, South Kensington.

He went to school at Northaw Place, Potters Bar. "There were a great many strange scholars there," he observed of this academy; even as a young boy he was peculiarly responsive to the quality of strangeness, to which, later on, he was to give dominant expression. At school he developed anæmia and rheumatic fever, which brought his formal education to an early end. This seeming catastrophe turned out to be of the utmost value to his growth as an artist, for it enabled him, from his fourteenth year, to devote the whole of his energies to drawing, painting and the enlargement of his imaginative experience. The painters of the past owed a great part of their dexterity and resource to the length of their apprenticeship; at the age when the art student of to-day begins his education, his predecessor had mastered the elements of his craft, and often considerably more. Illness had a further and not less important effect upon Burra's career. In other circumstances his parents might well have opposed his adopting a vocation which offered such uncertain prospects, but in their anxiety concerning his health they welcomed his interest in the arts. But he began to draw some time before his illness, and his earliest subject, the

crowded interior of a bus, contains the essence of one which has much occupied him since: people in public places.

Two years after leaving school he entered the Chelsea Polytechnic, where he worked from 1921 until 1923. After spending a further year as a student at the Royal College of Art, he returned to his father's house at Rye.

Not sufficiently robust to stand for long periods at a stretch ("I must sit most of the time; if I could work lying down I'd do so," he explained), he finds water-colour the most convenient medium, which, especially of recent years, he has often employed upon a colossal scale. After he was a student he never used a model; he works always from memory or imagination. It is his practice to begin a picture by making an elaborate pencil drawing of his subject (see Plate 26) which he then entirely covers with water-colour, thickly applied.

In the nineteen-twenties he made, for their

own sake, a large number of delicate, incisive pencil drawings, but most of his more recent work in this medium has constituted merely the foundation of his finished pictures.

He works every day, morning and afternoon. Almost the sole interruptions in this strict manner of existence are his visits abroad. There is a story, current among his friends, that one evening he went out, telling his mother he was going into the garden. When night came he had not returned. Nor was there any sign of him next day or for many days. Then one evening, six months later, he walked into the house as though he had just left it. It transpired that all this time he had been living in New York, making drawings of Negro dives in Harlem. When questioned as to the truth of this story, he admitted that it was not entirely apocryphal, but, apocryphal or not, the story is psychologically true.

In addition to making drawings and paintings Burra has designed the scenery and costumes for three ballets, *Rio Grande*, produced by the Camargo Society in 1931, *Barabau* and *The Miracle in the Gorbals*, performed by the Sadler's Wells Company in 1938 and 1944.

Apart from these two ventures, which brought him momentarily into public notice, Burra lives in jealously-guarded seclusion. Only on rare occasions are his pictures to be seen in exhibitions, for he is as nearly indifferent as an artist can reasonably be to the public's opinion of his work. This indifference is due, I believe, not to any sense of superiority, but to the realization that, on account of the frailty of his health, his strength is barely sufficient to enable him to do his work, and he has no superabundance to spare for the politics of art, or for dispensable personal relations. From time to time he contributes (generally under mild protest) to exhibitions, and he has held three one-man shows: two at the Leicester Galleries—in April, 1929, and in May, 1932—and a third at the Redfern Gallery in

November and December 1942. And he was concerned, at least nominally, in one collective enterprise; he accepted membership of Unit I, a group of eleven artists—architects, sculptors and painters—founded in 1933, of whom the moving spirit was Paul Nash, one of his earliest supporters.

But notwithstanding the admiration of such artists as John and Nash, his membership of so distinguished—and so well publicized—a group as Unit I, and his haunting vision and unquestionable powers, Burra has made little impression either upon public, critics or collectors. So far as I have been able to ascertain, with the exception of two very brief notes[1] (and occasional, though mostly respectful, references in press reviews of exhibitions), nothing has been written about this artist's work.

[1] Foreword by Hugh Blaker to a catalogue of Paintings by E. J. Burra (The Leicester Galleries, April 1929); and Edward Burra, a note by Douglas Cooper in *Unit I*, "An Account of the Modern Movement in English Architecture, Painting and Sculpture," edited by Herbert Read (Cassell, 1934).

Such are the principal outward events of Burra's life. Because he is sedentary from necessity and unremittingly industrious from choice, these lack colour and movement, and give no indication of the rare quality of his imagination. A visit to his studio, even apart from the opportunities there to be found of studying his work, might perhaps be the best revelation of his mind, containing, as it does, a profusion of evidence as to the sources of his vision.

The publication, *Unit I*, contains photographs of the studio of each member of the group. The aspect of Burra's studio must have been altered by the accumulations of the past ten years; for the photograph gives an impoverished impression of this remarkable place. Its effect upon the visitor is enhanced by the contrasting character of the remainder of the house. It is a solid house, built about a century ago, in the box-shape favoured by the architects active under William IV. The massiveness of the building, the respectable character of the landscapes ("the colour of old violins") on the walls of hall and staircase, and of the Victorian water-colours in the drawing-room, the well-kept and symmetrically disposed furniture, are comfortable and reassuring. The visitor, as he emerges from these surroundings into the studio (which is situated at the top of the house among the servants' bedrooms), finds there no comfort or assurance. The walls are covered with vast numbers of photographs of Greek sculptures, paintings by Tiepolo, Signorelli, Magnasco and the Spanish masters, and with pictures clipped from newspapers—English, French, Spanish, Italian—of dramatic incidents and vivid poses. One of these shows the face of a leper, close up. Covering the floor, the wireless, the gramophone, and the chairs are many hundreds of books and magazines: there are novels in several languages, South American picture papers, Victorian scrap-books, and volumes of Elizabethan poetry and drama. Among these are numbers of gramophone records, for Burra listens to music while he works (Berlioz is his favourite composer). And on top of this profusion are scattered numerous white paper cylinders, which prove to be Burra's water-colour drawings, curled up. None of his own works is hung, but a few, returned from exhibitions, lean framed against the walls.

A moment's examination of these extraordinary pictures, many of them enormous, charged with energy, menace and conflict, in relation to the ubiquitous reproductions, should be sufficient to convince the spectator that, however freely Burra may borrow from other artists, he invariably remains himself.

The early ending of his formal education allowed him to read, in place of classics and mathematics, the books required to enrich his visual imagination. These were, in the main, books read by the cosmopolitan world of

Montparnasse, the works, for instance, of Pierre Macorlan, of Francis Carco, of Blaise Cendras, of Daniel Fuchs. He also read much Dickens, and, more significantly, novels of horror such as Horace Walpole's *Castle of Otranto* and Harrison Ainsworth's *Tower of London*. He was soon widely read in Elizabethan literature. For the works of Tourneur, and of Marston—his *Scourge of Villanie*, in particular—he conceived a lasting admiration. Nor was he slow to discover books by the older French and Spanish authors characterized by the same *terribilità*.

Of painting his knowledge was not less precocious. Caran d'Ache and Gustave Doré were his earliest favourites, but Tiepolo he claims for his most enduring passion—a platonic passion, it would seem, for I have been able to detect no trace of the Tiepolesque spirit in his work. But his debts to Signorelli, El Greco, Zurbarán, and above all to Goya, are conspicuous. From Signorelli he learnt the effectiveness of hard,

simple modelling, and of the taut pose in conveying the suggestion of restrained violence; to his debt to Spanish masters I shall refer later. Among his contemporaries, those who have contributed most to his ever receptive vision are Picasso, Georg Grosz, Chirico, Wyndham Lewis, Covarrubias and Dali.

But however often he may imitate other artists, it cannot be denied, even by someone to whom his art makes no appeal, that Burra's is a sensationally original vision. It is his awareness of his own inalienably personal quality which allows him, with perfect impunity, to study minutely the works of other highly personal, even of highly mannered artists, and to take from them whatever may serve his turn.

. . . .

It is melancholy to reflect upon the large number of artists who fail to fulfil the promise of their youth. "How easy to have talent when one is sixteen," Degas was fond of saying, "but how difficult when one is sixty." Whether British artists have manifested, during the past century, a particular inability to stay the course, I would hesitate to say, but it is beyond dispute that the number in whom the first fine careless rapture has been chilled by premature senility is large. How often does some unsigned painting by which we have been captivated turn out to be an early work of an artist with the complacent dull-eyed productions of whose later years we are already too familiar. The catastrophic deterioration of Millais's genius —which is apt to be regarded as the penalty paid by a stainless pre-Raphaelite for his uniquely iniquitous compact with Mammon—exemplifies, in its extremist form, a tendency from which only the very wise and the young in heart appear immune. That Burra's richly imaginative art, far from manifesting symptoms of settling, is obviously and securely in the process of acquiring an enhanced resonance and breadth, strengthens my belief that he is a painter of exceptional stature.

It was in the early nineteen-twenties that I first saw Burra's work, and met, from time to time, the artist himself, a student retiring in disposition and delicate in health. In those days he was a silent, pale boy, who put me in mind of a machine which had almost run down, so near did his small reserve of energy seem to exhaustion.

It was apparent from the pencil drawings of nudes he made at the Chelsea Polytechnic and the Royal College of Art—elaborate studies, finished with a kind of astringent suavity—how accomplished he already was, for the best of them revealed a searching sense of form. The small figure compositions to which he gave the greater part of his time seemed to me to afford less evidence of exceptional talent; they had the same exquisite finish as the nudes, but they were a belated and sterile flowering of *art nouveau*, a deft but arbitrary blend of the mannerisms from Aubrey Beardsley, Walter Crane, Caran d'Ache and Edmund Dulac. But it was not long before Burra discovered the subject which, for the ensuing fifteen years, he took as his special province: the underworld of Latin Europe. And he treated it, from the first, with sovereign confidence. It is characteristic of him that he did not wait until he had visited the Continent before portraying, with a profusion of detail, various aspects of its low life.

There was something most bizarre in the contrast between the sedate existence of this delicate, home-loving schoolboy, and the products of his imagination: nocturnal street encounters in the red-light districts of Continental cities, scenes in the tough water-side joints and in the sailors' brothels of Mediterranean ports. These places are portrayed with meticulous correctness; for Burra was not only acquainted with picaresque literature in more than one language, but, like

Utrillo, he made extensive use of picture post-cards, and in search of useful portrayals of underworld "types" or of characteristic interiors or costumes he frequented purveyors of that kind of card most likely to provide the required material. But it is not, of course, to their accuracy that Burra's scenes of low life owe their uniqueness, but to his almost preternatural comprehension of haunts of corruption. I question whether his pictures of these do not constitute the most grand and the most vivid interpretations of the least reputable seams of society by any painter of our time.

Early in life Burra experienced, in its most acute form, the northerner's usual nostalgia for the Latin South. "I've never been even faintly curious about any northern country, but I've wanted, as long as I can remember, to go to Mexico and Venice," I heard him declare. He paid the first of many visits to Paris in the early nineteen-twenties, and with his increasing knowledge of France his treatment of his chosen subjects assumed an ever richer variety.

It is no longer necessary to ask why Burra should have devoted his rare talents to subjects in themselves often squalid and corrupt. This is, in any case, a question not easy, perhaps even impossible, to answer precisely. As will already be apparent, he was early fascinated by low life. As the direction of the satire in his underworld pictures testifies, he is far from complacent towards evil, yet on the balance it attracted more than it repelled him. Delight in the disreputable haunts which, for about fifteen years, constituted the principal sources of his inspiration—delight in their grotesqueness, their sinister ambience, and their flamboyance, was the most positive element in Burra's art. Throughout that time the underworld was the place where his imagination was stimulated to its highest pitch.

One of the most marked characteristics of Burra's treatment of his subject is the tendency to specialize he showed from the first. A particular aspect of the underworld was his peculiar province. Except when, under the spell of Georg Grosz' cynical, fleshy profiteers, he momentarily turned his attention to its more luxurious manifestations, he has shown a consistent preference for the disreputable in its most meretricious aspects. What other artist can portray, so exactly, for example, the exuberant cut and fibrous texture of cheap clothes?

For Burra, a member of a prosperous and respected family, brought up in South Kensington and in the solid, reassuring house at Rye, the garish resorts which figure in his pictures have probably the tantalizing attractiveness of the utterly remote. Artists are continually enlarging our conception of the beautiful, by including in its canon subjects from which preceding generations averted their gaze. (It was not so long ago that all but the most ceremonious aspects of contemporary life were held to be unworthy of the attention of the practitioner of "High Art".) It has remained for Burra to create, out of the flashy decoration of the *boîte*, a new rococo which has a copious and exotic grandeur and the deliquescent fantasy which belongs to dreams.

The characters which people Burra's pictures of this period, corrupt though they mostly appear, are less active protagonists of evil than pitiful creatures, the self-murderers, the morally infirm, the predestined victims of every evil spirit which walks the earth for the ruin of souls. There is something childlike about even the most sinister among them. The young man in *Café* (Plate 16), who sits in slyly smiling meditation upon some unlawful pleasure or nefarious scheme, although he is evidently in the highest degree susceptible to temptation, is not innately or determinedly evil. His characters' moral infirmities Burra depicts with a relish so remorseless as to make the squeamish wince, but he has sympathy for the love of personal independence which even the weakest of them shares, and he is fascinated by the bizarre pattern of their lives as they move, through the warm and relaxing atmosphere of self-indulgence, towards an awaiting nemesis.

In spite of his somewhat cloistered life, and his merely fitful interest in public affairs, Burra is peculiarly responsive to the dominant currents of thought and feeling which agitate the world at large. The paintings on which he was engaged between the early nineteen-twenties and the later nineteen-thirties reveal his at once painful and ravished awareness of the moral state of Europe. These pictures constitute a remarkably faithful interpretation of certain of the moods—the indecision and the lethargy, the disillusionment and the restlessness—which prevailed between the wars. But with the assumption of power by the Nazis in 1933 the world was faced with a simple and momentous issue, and, albeit too slowly, people began to understand that they must either submit to slavery, or fight to preserve their liberties. The new and graver mood was crystallized by the Civil War in Spain. This terrible struggle seized the imagination of the world. On the eve of the cataclysm Burra happened to be in Madrid. "One day when I was lunching with some Spanish friends," he told me, "smoke kept blowing by the restaurant window. I asked where it came from. 'Oh, it's nothing,' someone answered with a shade of impatience, 'it's only a church being burnt!' That made me feel sick. It was terrifying: constant strikes, churches on fire, and pent-up hatred everywhere: everybody knew that something appalling was just about to happen."

The Spanish Civil War had an immediate and radical effect upon Burra's art. From then on, it was characterized by a more solemn note, and tragedy upon a more exalted level became his constant theme.

The event had not found Burra unprepared.

For several years before the outbreak of the Civil War he had been under the spell of Spain: he had studied, with intense excitement, El Greco, Zurbarán and Goya, and the dramatic and luxuriant (and in England very little known) architecture and sculpture of the Jesuit Baroque churches of Mexico. He taught himself Spanish (by the Hugo method), and visited both Mexico and Spain. He came to take an equal delight in luxuriant Mexico and in withered and exalted Castile.

On a recent visit to his studio I was inspecting a number of his works, and there was one which I wished to see a second time—"a big scene reminding me of the Conquistador period of Spanish history" was how I described it. We recovered the painting in question, which depicted a group of soldiers whose clothes and surroundings bore a marked sixteenth-century aspect. "Oh! *that* was the one you wanted, was it?" he said; "but it's of *this* war: those are

British soldiers, just outside Rye." "But this, surely," I said, indicating a vast building with its great windows magnificently barred, "can't be anything but a Spanish palace."

"I suppose it is," he replied. "I must have copied it from a postcard I brought back from Spain."

· · · · ·

Burra's scenes from the life of the underworld are charged with a rich though sinister poetry, but in comparison with the best of his more recent works they seem almost frivolous; for the former are conceived on an altogether grander scale. Just as the pictures of low life reflect something profoundly characteristic of the immediate past, so do these later pictures reflect the prevailing sense of the im-

minence of vast issues, and of vast catastrophes.

The last decade has been remarkable for a resurgence of the imaginative impulse in British painting. Of this resurgence the finest of Burra's pictures, such, for instance, as *Mexican Church* (Plate 27), *Soldiers* (Plate 25), *War in the Sun* (Plate 31), and *Bal des Pendues* (Plate 29), are likely to rank among the most memorable manifestations. He is without Moore's sanity and grasp of monumental form, or Sutherland's disturbing perception of obscure correspondences between the emotions and certain forms in Nature, Bawden's exquisite astringency, or Ravilious's elegance and impeccable sense of design, yet in the intensity and grandeur of his apprehension of the great drama now being enacted Burra stands alone.

John Rothenstein

Plate 1 FORTUNE TELLERS. 1929

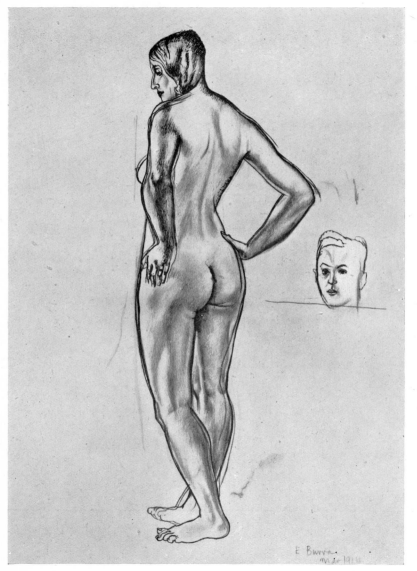

E Burra.
Mar 1924

Plate 2 LIFE STUDY. 1924

Plate 3 THE TORTURERS. 1935

Plate 4   DANCING GIRLS IN TOP HATS.   1928

Plate 5   ROSSI.   1930

Plate 6 NIGHT CLUB. 1930

Plate 7   Las Folies de Belleville.   1928

Plate 8　The Sisters.　1929

Plate 9 THE TERRACE. 1927

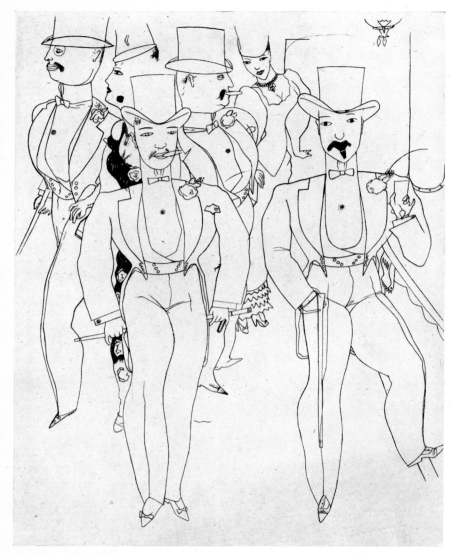

Plate 10 Dandies. 1930

Plate 11   HARLEM.   1936

Plate 12 John Deth. 1932

Plate 13 THE POINTING FINGER. 1937

Plate 14 DANCING COWS. 1933

Plate 15 ON THE SHORE. 1934

Plate 16 THE CAFÉ. 1932

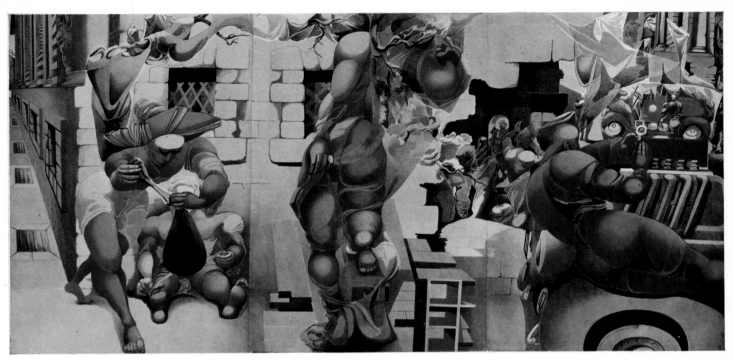

Plate 17 CAMOUFLAGE. 1938

Plate 18 DUENNAS. 1934

Plate 19 THE PUPPET. 1937

Plate 20 SILENCE. 1936

Plate 21 LANDSCAPE WITH WHEELS. 1937

Plate 22 BLASTED OAK. 1937

Plate 23 Blue-Robed Figure Under Tree. 1937

Plate 24   HOLY WEEK: SEVILLE.   1938

Plate 25   SOLDIERS.   1942

Plate 26 THE VISION OF ST. THERESA. 1938

Plate 27 MEXICAN CHURCH. 1938

Plate 28 THE WAKES. 1937

Plate 29 BAL DES PENDUES. 1937

Plate 30 THE RIOT. 1939

Plate 31   WAR IN THE SUN.   1938

Plate 32 AGONY IN THE GARDEN. 1936